Becalmed upon the sea of Thought,
Still unattained the land it sought,
My mind, with loosely-hanging sails,
Lies waiting the auspicious gales.

On either side, behind, before,
The ocean stretches like a floor,—
A level floor of amethyst,
Crowned by a golden dome of mist.

Blow, breath of inspiration, blow!
Shake and uplift this golden glow!
And fill the canvas of the mind
With wafts of thy celestial wind.

Henry Wadsworth Longfellow
In the Harbor, "Becalmed"

Barbara Ernst Prey

Reflections

BARBARA ERNST PREY

REFLECTIONS

Essay by Paul Lieberman

Reflections: Barbara Ernst Prey

Printed in China by C & C Offset Printing, Inc.
ISBN-10 1-42430-403-2 / ISBN-13 978-1-42430-403-5

Paul Lieberman is the Cultural Correspondent for the *Los Angeles Times*.

www.barbaraprey.com

Cover: *The Simple Life*, 2004, watercolor on paper, 28 x 39 inches

TABLE OF CONTENTS

Reflections: Thirty Years of Painting
by Barbara Ernst Prey

H ER NEW PAINTING FOR NASA, *SHUTTLE DISCOVERY: RETURN TO FLIGHT*, WAS ON AN EASEL, WAITING TO BE UNVEILED, WHEN BARBARA ERNST PREY DISCUSSED HER LIFE AND WORK WITH PAUL LIEBERMAN, THE ROVING CULTURAL CORRESPONDENT OF THE LOS ANGELES TIMES. THIS IS DRAWN FROM THAT JANUARY 18, 2006 CONVERSATION AT THE WILLIAMS CLUB IN NEW YORK.

Paul Lieberman: A couple of summers ago, my wife and I were driving up to Maine to see friends and decided to make a detour to Port Clyde, where Barbara has a studio. You have to go to the middle of nowhere, out onto a point. She has a gallery downstairs and then you head up to her work area, next to a deck that provides views of the fishing shacks she paints and the harbor where Edward Hopper used to take a boat out to the islands and where one of the Wyeths still eats lunch at a dockside café. She was perched on a beautiful spot.

Then a couple of Saturdays ago, we went out to Oyster Bay to see her home there, an old Victorian house that Teddy Roosevelt had something to do with building, and once again you have to climb up high to see where she paints, in another studio with views of an historic waterfront. It's easy to be jealous of someone who works in those circumstances and then you hear that she is going to Paris and Madrid where American embassies are displaying her work. It's no fair.

But I saw something else in that studio that made any jealousy vanish—a blank canvas. It was a reminder that all the artist has to do is muster up the courage and vision to create something out of nothing, then do it again and do it again. That's all.

So, to start, I gather that you grew up with a painter in the house.

Barbara Prey: Yes. My mother was head of the Design Department at Pratt Art Institute (fig. 1). She was an incredible painter and she had a large studio in our home. I remember she always had the opera on Saturdays, and she'd have a still life set up so I could just draw or paint. She was a quiet role model. I thought that everyone grew up as I did.

P: Did she give you the brush or did you ask for the brush?

B: She didn't give me any instruction. I think art is something that calls you. It is in your genetic makeup. You can fight it, but eventually you circle back to your calling.

P: She painted in what medium?

B: She painted primarily in oils, but she was an exquisite draftsman and her pastels and watercolors are also excellent. She'd paint anything, though—the walls of our house, the furniture, even the trees in our backyard. She was having a party and down the hill was a gray birch. She didn't like it, so she painted it white. The vista needed a little white.

fig. 1

I didn't paint the trees, but started to paint in watercolors when I was maybe 14, 15. I've been painting in watercolors for close to 35 years and painting for more than 40.

P: Other than your mother, who else influenced you early on?

B: Over the years there have been many. Hopper was one early influence. In high school, I did a painting of our Main Street in the style of his painting at the Whitney, *Early Sunday Morning*. And Winslow Homer, who perhaps has been the strongest influence as his watercolors are so compelling. That's why it was so special to be asked by Frank Kelly, Curator of American and British Paintings at The National Gallery of Art in Washington, D.C. to give a lecture there this winter on "The Watercolors of Winslow Homer" for the Homer exhibit at the museum.

I studied art history at Williams College and later at Harvard, and was fortunate to study with remarkable people including Lane Faison, my mentor, who has been a great supporter of my work. I also was able to travel and see many great works of art while on a Fulbright Scholarship in Europe and later on a grant from The Henry Luce Foundation in Asia. Dürer was an early influence both for his watercolors and his etchings. Van Eyck, Medieval manuscripts, Mogul painting, Degas, the Luminists and a number of American painters I count as influences.

Of course, my first job after college did not involve painting. I did line drawings for the New Yorker, the New York Times and other publications. I bought our first dining room table, a side table, by doing illustrations for Gourmet magazine. But I was painting at night and on weekends.

P: When you decided to spend time in Maine, was that by chance or was it a sort of romantic act, because artists such as Hopper had been there—the equivalent of a writer going to Key West because Hemingway hung out there?

B: A good friend invited me to come to Maine when I was 18. I was taken with the landscape and the beauty and started to paint. She curated my first show in Maine and this year it will be 30 years of exhibiting in Maine. Maine was such an inspiration for me that I kept coming back. I then discovered that my family roots not only go back to Maine in the 1700s but to the area where I love to paint. In fact a number of harbors and coves and land are named after them. It's a bit eerie if you think about it, it's like coming home but not even knowing.

P: What were the first things you painted?

B: Perhaps the dories. They were new for me and I was fascinated by their shapes, reflections and lines, but also with their history and connection to the sea. They are a symbol of a way of life, a point in time. In our age of technology, the beauty of the dories is that they are handcrafted.

To me they are an aesthetic object in themselves. But they were also fishing boats and a metaphor for the harshness of the fishing life. A lobster fisherman friend, Sherwood Cook, had a beautiful dory that I used to paint and I have a model he made of it to scale which I use for some of my paintings.

P: When we see a boat we easily think of the person who uses it, right?

B: Right. Oftentimes I know the people. Or, if it is a house, I know the people who live inside. So for me it is a type of portrait, it's not just the house. It's the personal connection to the house, the inside and outside.

After the dories, I began a quilt series. We lived in western Pennsylvania for about ten years, at the foothills of Appalachia, and I would drive around in the hollows and very rural areas in search of painting ideas. What I thought was beautiful, the character of the run-down houses was, of course, poverty. There was a group of 80-year-olds who met in our church once a week and quilted. They raised their children on rural farms, worked hard and had tough lives. Quilting was their weekly social event. The quilters made us a beautiful patchwork quilt that I painted in *Americana*. I was in Maine a couple of years later and came upon a group of quilts out on a line, supported by sticks, blowing in the wind. That began the quilt series of paintings. The idea had been with me for quite some time, it just needed that visual impetus to take shape. The quilts are so American and, again, something we are losing, the tie to the land and our collective history. In our technically connected, wired world they represent human interaction, creativity, community and craftsmanship. Like the dories, the quilts are a metaphor, a sort of portrait.

P: So were there actually quilts hanging outside those Maine houses?

B: Yes and no. Oftentimes they weren't there. *Reunion* and *Reunion at Dusk* are two large paintings with quilts. *Reunion at Dusk* was on exhibit at the United States Embassy in Prague through the U.S. State Department's Arts in Embassies Program. In both paintings I put the quilts in because the composition needed something on the right as a balance.

P: How long do your love affairs with these symbols last? With the dories, for instance, or the quilts?

B: It depends—until I feel I'm finished with the subject. The quilts at first were about both the quilts and the quilters and the stories behind the quilts, portraits of these women I really came to enjoy. Now the quilts are more in the background in my paintings. Maybe it's something I don't quite want to let go of.

P: Then the Adirondack chairs start to appear. Now is this one of your 9/11 paintings?

B: *Ladies in Red* was the last I did before 9/11. The chairs were out on the lawn on Monhegan Island, just like that. Sometimes I'll rearrange things. Even with the White House Christmas card, we rearranged the furniture to make a better composition. But after 9/11, I couldn't paint. I was living on Long Island and, like everyone there, felt directly affected. I questioned whether what I did was significant in the grand scheme of things. I went back to the chair theme and reworked it, but called the painting *Waiting*.

P: We see the chairs and obviously we see the people, or the people who are no longer there after 9/11.

B: Yes, it's called *Waiting* because we were waiting to hear who was killed in the attacks and who was able to get out. There were a lot of unsubstantiated rumors.

P: That's a powerful metaphor and an easy one to grasp. I know it's an odd thing to ask, but do you ever second-guess whether your symbols are too graspable? You know, like music that is very narrative?

B: No, because that period of time was so powerful.

P: Now you could have gone and done a whole year of chairs after 9/11. But instead you turned to something that was much more risky. You started painting flags.

B: Yes. I happened to be driving over the bridge in New York and could see the Twin Towers burning. I learned that forty people from my hometown were killed. As you recall, flags were everywhere. After the attack, I went up to Maine for inspiration. Out of the corner of my eye, I saw a flag wrapped around the banister of an old Finnish church. That flag became a symbol of grief for my friend, the family left behind and others killed on 9/11. I continued with the flag series as a way of mourning and showing solidarity.

This painting *God and Country,* from the 9/11 series, is on exhibit at the U.S. Embassy in Paris. It's a close-up of an old church door on an island off the coast of Maine. I was just in Paris and the painting hangs in the entryway. I am the only living painter on exhibit with American artists including Sargent, Homer, Ryder, Hassam and Twachtman. You never know where things will end up. Other paintings from the 9/11 series are on exhibit at the American Embassy in Madrid, where I also just gave a lecture for their art collection opening.

P: Are the embassies in Paris and Madrid the first to show your work?

B: No. My work is on or has been exhibited at the United States Embassy in Prague, Minsk, Liberia and Oslo where I was invited by Ambassador Ong to give a joint presentation with him to the Norwegian business community on "Businesses Supporting the Arts." Ambassador Ong was the former President of the Business Committee for the Arts, founded by David

Rockefeller. On this recent trip to speak at the openings of the art collections at the U.S. Embassies in Paris and Madrid I was also invited to speak at the Thyssen-Bornemisza Museum about the American artists Homer and Hopper and their influence in my work.

P: Still, getting back to painting flags-it is tricky. I wrote about their power too in the wake of 9/11. My wife and I drove up to New England on my first day off after weeks of being around death in the city and everywhere along those country roads the flags were out. I was brought up in an era when we were suspicious of flag-waving, but it was very reassuring that people in so-called "heartland communities" cared so much about what had happened in New York. For an artist, however, it's now 50 years since Jasper Johns painted his flag and supposedly took away its power, turned it into just another object.

B: I grew up seeing his flag painting at MoMA. But to me the flag was a metaphor. Seeing the little flags in the windows was telling a story as opposed to flag waving. I like the concept of image as insight. It gives us insight into a particular time—the image had such a different connotation at that point, five years ago, than it does today. So these paintings are actually time-sensitive, hermeneutical.

fig. 2

P: Then you were asked to do the White House Christmas card (fig. 2). Did you have the option of painting an exterior or interior?

B: Yes I did. We began with an exterior idea and I did drawings on the front lawn and on the back lawn. Then the First Lady decided to go with an interior scene.

P: I'm sure that's a commission you can't turn down. At the same time, that seems like an uncomfortable thing for you to do, to suddenly paint an interior. It is not the natural "you."

B: It's exciting and uncomfortable at the same time because you are painting the Christmas card for the White House that is sent to heads of state around the world. I was told the painting becomes a national treasure and is in the permanent collection of the White House. My painting is of the Diplomatic Reception Room and yes, it pushed me in different ways.

P: It must have been similar when you got the call from NASA. I mean, there was a reason you were drawn to paint dories, quilts and houses. But spaceships! Did you have to reach to find your heart in those? Then there are the technical issues—we don't see much black in your Maine scenes.

B: Correct. These are all painted with watercolors, which is a transparent medium, so the challenge was to make the sky a dense black. The International Space Station was my first of four NASA commissions and is on exhibit at the Kennedy Space Center. It was commissioned three years ago, but the International Space Station isn't finished. So there was only a small little section from which to work. NASA sent me photos and I set up a model. I also went down to NASA and saw some of the parts. I spent six months doing research as I like to know all about something before I paint it. It was the same with the quilts and dories. For the quilts, I visited the annual Mennonite Quilt Sale in Indiana to examine their quilts. Then I come back, process everything and come up with my own voice. I am pleased with the International Space Station painting because I created something that wasn't there.

The black background was a challenge, but I used many different colors. There are reds, blues, greens and blacks in there, all these layers of colors to make it opaque. Then the stars—that was really fun. I was mixing many different pigments—five different types of gold, copper, silver— some of them toxic. It is a painting of combined medium on paper. The atmosphere is pastel and there are different pastels in the sky. It was a challenge and I probably spent much more time learning about space than painting.

P: It may be my imagination, but I think these space paintings, especially the first ones, were problematic for you. It was hard to make them your own. And all the while they're paying you almost nothing for this struggle.

B: Yes, but it's the challenge and the honor of being a NASA artist with the likes of Norman Rockwell, Andy Warhol and Robert Rauschenberg. My two paintings of the *International Space Station* and the *Columbia Tribute* painting are on exhibit at the Kennedy Space Center, next to Warhol's NASA commission. *The Discovery: Return to Flight* painting will go on a national tour (fig. 3).

P: That they kept calling you back speaks for itself. But to paint a tribute to a fallen crew could not have been easy.

B: Yes, NASA usually commissions one artist per project but they liked my work so much that they've commissioned me four times. After the *International Space Station* came the *Columbia Tribute* and the *X-43*, a painting of the fastest aircraft in the world. NASA sent me out to the Mohave Desert to the launch. The challenge with the *Columbia Tribute* was to do something that would honor the astronauts' families because NASA unveiled the painting at the anniversary dinner at the Air and Space Museum in Washington, D.C. and presented prints of the painting to the families. That was a moving moment for me. And now the *Discovery Shuttle: Return to Flight* painting. The Discovery painting was a companion painting to the Columbia, offering a sort of closure.

fig. 3

P: You went to the Discovery launch, correct?

B: NASA sent me photos, but I prefer to work from life. I was able to go down for the liftoff which was majestic. I saw the Discovery go up and up into the sky with a surreal reflection in the still water that was in front of me. No photograph could have captured that image or the spirit of the moment, and it was important for me to be able to experience that for the painting. I tried to connect the Columbia with the Discovery in the reflection. I am an academic at heart and all of these NASA commissions were fascinating. Not only did they challenge me creatively but they expanded my world intellectually.

P: As I told you when I first saw that painting in your home, I think that you found yourself in that one—you finally found a way to make the spacecraft paintings your own. But what's most intriguing is how these commissions outside your comfort zone seem to have had an impact on the work for which you are best known. Am I crazy, or is there a correlation between your having to do an interior of the White House, then going back to Maine and doing more interiors, except now you take us inside fishermen's shacks.

B: Last year I began to explore the theme 'Works on Water' and did a show of that title in Maine which will travel to New York this fall. There is an insightful catalog essay by Sarah Cash, the Corcoran Gallery of Art curator in the accompanying book. The interior idea, which you pointed out, ties in with the White House Christmas card. I am sure that was part of the unconscious thought process. Oftentimes my paintings incubate for three to ten years, or even longer. I will see something and then think about it and how I would paint it. I've been watching the life and work of fishermen for the 30 years I've been painting in Maine. They are my neighbors and friends. I've painted the boats, but I really haven't explored the life. It's very different than the tourist's romanticized image, it's a harsh life. There is a raw, tough, ugly side to it. That is what I wanted to examine. In fact, I've explored the Maine coast and made multiple trips to Nova Scotia to research this theme. It's like the quilts and the NASA work—there's a long thinking period before the work appears.

The lives shown are a contrast to those lived by my cerebral neighbors here in New York who may fly to Asia or Europe for work, live on their cell phones, BlackBerries and computers and are tied to the financial world. These fishermen work manually. Their office is the sea and their product is tangible. They are directly connected with nature and their craft is making their buoys, fixing their traps, mending the nets. The lobstermen are like our farmers, working the land or sea for their livelihood. But human nature is human nature. They compete just like the New York business crowd. This fisherman in *Blue Note* (pg. 73) also had a sense of humor and was artistic in making his buoys. They're his quilts. You see the beer bottles in his workshop. He's painting the buoys and having a beer. I'm capturing a snapshot of the life.

P: Did you meet him?

B: No. His building is owned by someone I know, so they let me in. He knows what I did, yes. But I try to observe from afar. I almost don't want the contact. I feel I'm still exploring the life, and the contact would change the story. I'm not ready to put a period at the end of that sentence. And if he knows I'm coming he might pretty up the workshop.

P: OK, so here you're doing interiors. Then we see this other new painting from Maine, of a house on a hill, and the sky is different than before—more solid—and the house looks ready to blast off. Tell me that's not the influence of your space paintings.

B: You're referring to *The Simple Life* (pg. 31) which does have a sky similar to the Discovery painting. Interestingly, I hadn't painted clear blue skies for a number of years. I was more interested in atmosphere and mood so my skies were dusk, or dark or foggy. I think it was after 9/11 that I returned to paint a stark blue sky, the color of the sky that day.

P: And if we make the trek out onto that point in Maine this summer, what new wrinkle will we see from Barbara Ernst Prey?

B: Well, I've actually done a couple of people. So that's unusual. *The Mender*, (pg. 39) is a fisherman mending his net. My husband Jeff said, "You didn't even define the face." When you get up close, there aren't any eyes. But it's a view from afar. He's in the shadows. I don't know. We'll see where that goes. I'm just beginning.

PLATES

THE APPRENTICE   2005, watercolor on paper, 21 x 28 inches

A WINTER'S PROJECT   2005, watercolor on paper, 28 x 39 inches

SANCTUM   2006, watercolor on paper, 20 x 28 inches

Barbara Ernst Prey

MORNING COMMUTE   2005, watercolor on paper, 12 x 16 inches

Barbara Ernst Prey

THE SIMPLE LIFE   2004, watercolor on paper, 28 x 39 inches

FIRST DAY   2006, watercolor on paper, 21 x 28 inches

Barbara Ernst Prey

I will look at cliffs and clouds

With quiet eyes,

Watch the wind bow down the grass,

And the grass rise.

Edna St. Vincent Millay
Afternoon on a Hill

WINDOW VIEW   2005, watercolor on paper, 16 x 12 inches

THE MENDER   2006, watercolor on paper, 20 x 27 inches

OLD SCHOOL   2006, watercolor on paper, 21 x 29 inches

Branch Hangers   2005, watercolor on paper, 21 x 28 inches

43

A WORK IN PROGRESS   2006, watercolor on paper, 20 x 28 inches

STILL WATER   2004, watercolor on paper, 21 x 28 inches

SOUL MATES   2003, watercolor on paper, 21 x 28 inches

"Wouldst thou,"—so the helmsman answered,
"Learn the secret of the sea?
Only those who brave its dangers
Comprehend its mystery!"

Henry Wadsworth Longfellow
The Secret of the Sea

CLIMBING ROSES   2005, watercolor on paper, 16 x 12 inches

Barbara Ernst Prey

THE COLLECTION   2005, watercolor on paper, 20 x 28 inches

FLUORESCENT BUOYS   2005, watercolor on paper, 28 x 19 inches

Barbara Ernst Prey

RETREAT   2005, watercolor on paper, 21 x 29 inches

Barbara Ernst Prey

It was a Maine lobster town—
each morning boatloads of hands
pushed off for granite
quarries on the islands,

and left dozens of bleak
white frame houses stuck
like oyster shells
on a hill of rock,

and below us, the sea lapped
the raw little match-stick
mazes of a weir,
where the fish for bait were trapped.

Remember?

Robert Lowell, *Water*

Separate Paths   2005, watercolor on paper, 27 x 40 inches

ISLAND FIELD   2005, watercolor on paper, 26 x 39 inches

GHOST HOUSE   2003, watercolor on paper, 21 x 28 inches

WET PAINT   2006, watercolor on paper, 11 x 15 inches

VANISHING POINT   2006, watercolor on paper, 26 x 38 inches

BLUE NOTE   2004, watercolor on paper, 21 x 27 inches

Biographical Notes,
Collections & Bibliography

1957   Born in New York City
1979   B.A., Williams College
1986   M.Div., Harvard Divinity School

Awards and Fellowships:
2004   New York State Senate Women of Distinction Award
1998   Artist in Residence, Westminster School, Simsbury, CT
1996   Best of Show, Westmoreland Museum of American Art
1986   Henry Luce Foundation Grant
1979   Fulbright Scholarship
1974   San Francisco Art Institute, Summer Grant

Listed:
Who's Who in the World
Who's Who in America, 50th Anniversary Edition
Who's Who of American Women
Who's Who in American Art

Selected Exhibitions:
2006   The White House
         United States Art in Embassies Program, U.S. Embassy, Paris, France
         United States Art in Embassies Program, U.S. Embassy, Madrid, Spain
         Kennedy Space Center, NASA Commission
         Chelsea Art Museum, New York, NY
         From Seacoast to Outer Space, The Williams Club, NY
         Guild Hall Museum, East Hampton, NY
         Lift Off, Vanderbilt Planetarium, NY
         Thirty Years of Painting Maine, Blue Water Fine Arts, Port Clyde, ME
2005   The White House
         United States Art in Embassies Program, U.S. Embassy, Oslo, Norway
         United States Art in Embassies Program, U.S. Embassy, Belarus
         United States Art in Embassies Program, U.S. Embassy, Liberia
         Kennedy Space Center, NASA Commission
         Guild Hall Museum, East Hampton, NY
         Works on Water, Blue Water Fine Arts, Port Clyde, ME
2004   The White House
         United States Art in Embassies Program, U.S. Embassy, Oslo, Norway
         United States Art in Embassies Program, U.S. Embassy, Belarus
         United States Art in Embassies Program, U.S. Embassy, Liberia

Kennedy Space Center, NASA Commission
Observations, Harrison Gallery, Williamstown, MA
Guild Hall Museum, East Hampton, NY
Conversations, Blue Water Fine Arts, Port Clyde, ME

2003   The White House
An American Portrait, Arts Club of Washington D.C.
United States Art in Embassies Program, U.S. Embassy, Prague
United States Art in Embassies Program, U.S. Embassy, Oslo, Norway
United States Art in Embassies Program, U.S. Embassy, Belarus
United States Art in Embassies Program, U.S. Embassy, Liberia

2003   Kennedy Space Center, NASA Commission
The Valley Viewed: 150 Years of Artists Exploring Williamstown,
     Harrison Gallery, Williamstown, MA Curated by Katherine Carroll
Guild Hall Museum, East Hampton, NY
National Arts Club, NY
25 Years of Painting Maine, Blue Water Fine Arts, Port Clyde, ME

2002   United States Art in Embassies Program, U.S. Embassy, Prague
United States Art in Embassies Program, U.S. Embassy, Oslo, Norway
Obsession, Heckscher Museum of Art, Huntington, NY
American Art in Miniature, Gilcrease Museum, Tulsa, OK
Guild Hall Museum, East Hampton, NY
Patriot, Blue Water Fine Arts, Port Clyde, ME
A Trace in the Mind: An Artists Response to 9/11, Hutchins Gallery, C.W.
     Post College, Brookville, NY

2001   *Lightscapes*, Jensen Fine Arts, New York City
Guild Hall Museum, East Hampton, NY
American Art in Miniature, Gilcrease Museum, Tulsa, OK
Recent Watercolors, Blue Water Fine Arts, Port Clyde, ME

2000   *American Art in Miniature*, Gilcrease Museum, Tulsa, OK

1999   *Recent Watercolors*, Jensen Fine Arts, New York City
Heckscher Museum, Huntington, NY
American Art in Miniature, Gilcrease Museum, Tulsa, OK
Guild Hall Museum, East Hampton, NY

1998   *American Art in Miniature*, Gilcrease Museum, OK
Express Yourself, Portland Museum of Art, ME

1997   Museum of the Southwest, Midland, TX
Recent Acquisitions, Farnsworth Museum of Art, Rockland, ME

1996   The Westmoreland Museum of American Art, Awarded *Best in Show*

1995   The Philadelphia Museum of Art

1994	Farnsworth Museum of Art Benefit Auction Exhibit, Rockland, ME
1993	Blair Art Museum, Hollidaysburg, PA
	Johnstown Art Museum, Johnstown, PA
1989	*Women's Art*, Williams College, Williamstown, MA
1988	Museum of Fine Arts, Nassau County, NY
1986	Harvard University, Cambridge, MA

Selected Collections:

President and Mrs. George Bush
President and Mrs. George W. Bush
The White House
The Farnsworth Art Museum
Williams College
Williams College Museum of Art
The Taiwan Museum of Art
Mellon Hall, Harvard Business School
The Henry Luce Foundation
Reader's Digest Corporation
Prince and Princess Castell
Prince and Princess Johannes Lobkowicz
Prince and Princess Michael Salm
Mrs. C. Robert Allen
Mr. Herbert Allen
Mr. and Mrs. James Broadhurst
Mr. Sam Bronfman
Mr. and Mrs. Russell Byers Jr.
Governor Hugh Carey
Mr. and Mrs. Chris Davis
Mr. and Mrs. Allan Fulkerson
Senator and Mrs. Judd Gregg
Mrs. Henry Luce III
Mr. and Mrs. Dan Lufkin
Mr. and Mrs. James McCarl
Mr. Richard P. Mellon
Mr. Roger Milliken
Ambassador and Mrs. John Ong
Mr. and Mrs. Peter O'Neill
Mr. and Mrs. Howard Phipps, Jr.
Ambassador and Mrs. Mitchell Reiss

Ambassador and Mrs. Craig Stapleton
Dr. and Mrs. James Watson
Mr. and Mrs. Jimmy Webb
Mrs. Libby Pataki, Office of the First Lady of New York

Selected Bibliography and Interviews:

Barbara Ernst Prey: Works on Water, essay by Corcoran Gallery of Art Curator Sarah Cash, 2005
Names and Faces: An Artist Ready for Liftoff, The Washington Post, July 22, 2005 (interview)
The Difference in Barbara Ernst Prey, Maine Sunday Telegram, August 28, 2005 (interview)
NPR, July 2005 (interview)
An Artist on a Space Mission, Newsday, July 17, 2005 (interview)
Footlights: Artist Shooting for the Stars, The New York Times, July 10, 2005. (interview)
Capturing the Moment, Florida Today, July 13, 2005 (interview)
On the Town, The New York Sun, April 15-17, 2005
2005 Women of Distinction, Distinction Magazine, March 2005 (interview)
Barbara Ernst Prey: Studio Visit, PBS WLIW- NY, January 2005
Painter Seeing a Bigger Picture, Los Angeles Times, October 4, 2004
Prey Exhibit in Maine, Coastal Living Magazine, Summer 2004
Columbia Tribute, CNN News with Carol Lin, February 2, 2004 (interview)
Columbia Tribute, CNN Newssource, February 1, 2004 (interview)
NPR, February 2004 (interview)
The Fine Art of the Space Age, The Washington Post, January 26, 2004
Artist Reaches New Heights, The Boston Globe, January 20, 2004
Tribute Reflects the Lives of Columbia Crew, Newsday, February 1, 2004
Artist Fulfills New Mission for NASA, AP Newswire, January 26, 2004
1010 Wins Radio New York with Joe Montone, February 1, 2004 (interview)
WOR The Ed Walsh Show, February 1, 2004 (interview)
Prey's Columbia Tribute, CBS News Radio, February 1, 2004 (interview)
White House Artist, Voice of America, December 4, 2004 (interview)
Talk of the Town, The New Yorker, December 1, 2003
She Answered a Call from Washington, The New York Times, December 21, 2003
CNN, Paula Zahn NOW, December 23, 2003 (interview)
Larry King Live, CNN, December 2003 (interview)
HGTV White House Christmas Special, December, 2003 (interview)
End Page: Barbara Ernst Prey, The Robb Report, August 2003, September 2003
Arts and Antiques Magazine, Summer 2003
A Trace in the Mind: An Artists Response to 9/11, catalog essay by Charles Riley, C.W. Post University
Public Lives, The New York Times, October 31, 2002
Williamstown Artist Compared to Homer, The Paper, November 29, 2002

On the Loose in New York, The International Art Newspaper, April 2001
Famous Last Words, Linda Stasi, The New York Post, April 22, 2001
The Critic's Choice, The New York Daily News, April 2001
The Joan Hamburg Show, April 2001 (interview)
True North: Barbara Ernst Prey Inspirations, Maine PBS, 2001 (interview)
Watercolor 2001: Barbara Ernst Prey New Work, American Artist Magazine 2001
Where Artists Live Their Work Comes Alive, Newsday, Annual Home Magazine Issue, Cover
PBS-Channel 21, The Metro Report, New York, June 1999 (interview)
The Critic's Choice, The New York Daily News, January 1999
Art Market: Prey Exhibit, The International Art Newspaper, January 1999
WOR-AM The Joan Hamburg Show (interview)
The Exchange with Channel 12, January 1999 (interview)
The Maine Focus: Barbara Ernst Prey, Interview with Andrew Bowser, WERU, October 7, 1997
Winners, Newsday, November 1996.
Career Moves: Two Successful Artists Offer Advice, American Artist Magazine, Watercolor 1991
Taiwan Pictured Through Western Eyes, Asia Magazine, July 1987
U.S. Painter Views Taiwan With Color and Contrast, China Post, May 1987

Artwork Commissions:
NASA Commission – 2005 Shuttle Relaunch
NASA Commission – 2005 The x-43
NASA Commission – 2005 International Space Station Print
NASA Commission – 2004 Columbia Commemorative
NASA Commission – 2004 International Space Station
White House Christmas Card, 2003

Lectures:
The National Gallery of Art, "The Watercolors of Winslow Homer"
U.S. Embassy, Oslo, "Business Supporting the Arts"
U.S. Embassy, Prague, "The 9/11 Series"
U.S. Embassy, Paris
U.S. Embassy, Madrid
Thyssen-Bornemisza Museum, Madrid

What seas what shores what grey rocks and what islands
What water lapping the bow
And scent of pine and the woodthrush singing through the fog
What images return

T.S. Eliot, *Marina*